Parenting the Bible Way

Parenting the Bible Way

the

SHERRY RONKE

PARENTING THE BIBLE WAY

iUniverse books may be ordered through booksellers or by contacting:

iUniverse
1663 Liberty Drive
Bloomington, IN 47403
www.iuniverse.com
1-800-Authors (1-800-288-4677)

ISBN: 978-1-5320-6378-7 (sc)
ISBN: 978-1-5320-6377-0 (e)

Library of Congress Control Number: 2019900947

Print information available on the last page.

iUniverse rev. date: 02/11/2019

Contents

Author's Note...vii

Acknowledgement..ix

Chapter 1   Introduction 1

Chapter 2   Parenting...5

Chapter 3   Training..43

Chapter 4   Relationships 69

Chapter 5   Christian Faith 78

Chapter 6   Conclusion 95

Author's Note

When we are committed to a lifestyle of dependency on God in all that we do, the Holy Spirit takes over and holds our hands every step of the way. There is no book big enough to hold or contain all the necessary steps and guidelines given to us by the Holy Spirit as He walks with us in achieving our goals. It will be volumes and volumes of books if these were to be written, and so this write up does not claim absolute knowledge of how to raise children using the biblical principles. It is the writer's suggestion that whatever knowledge the readers may gain from reading this book, should be used as a seed. If allowed in the readers' heart, the Holy Spirit will water the seed for increase. As the inner tuition is applied in child rearing, the children will turn out a true heritage of the Lord (Psalm 127:3) who will make the world a better place and go on to fulfill God's purpose for their lives and for the kingdom of God.

Acknowledgement

All glory be to God for His inspirations and lots of thanks to my family for their help in typing and editing.

Chapter 1

Introduction

The world after the fall of man in the garden of Eden could be describe as a fallen world due to the curse placed on the ground (Genesis 3) by God. Naturally, whatever is left unattended will go from good to bad and bad to worse, order to disorder, beautiful to ugly. In short, things don't get better on their own. It takes constant attention and care to keep our lives in order. We engage in constant maintenance culture to keep our properties and materials in good shape. For example, if you keep a machine or a car unattended to for several years, at some point it will become a useless garbage without value. If we don't keep our yard groomed, the whole property will soon be overgrown with weeds and bushes that will invite dangerous animals to pay us visits. There is a biblical way to handle each aspect of our lives including raising our children.

Raising our children "the bible way" should be as normal as anything else in our lives. As Christians, our hearing God. The difference will be in our hearing ability, and being able to follow His instructions consistently. So, get to work and be ready to yield to the leading of the Holy Spirit step by step.

Chapter 2

Parenting

What is parenting?

It simply means child rearing. It is the primary job of the biological parents and many times with the participation of other people. Often times other people are involved for support or even to take over the complete responsibilities of the care of the child, depending on the circumstances. You may have situations where the mother is the major player, or the father is the major caregiver. Many times there are situations in which other agents are involved; examples are adoption, foster care, government, orphanage or other family members. The condition will dictate.

The process of parenting runs through infancy to adulthood. Every aspect of the child's life is touched, the physical, emotional, social, intellectual, and more importantly the spiritual development. A mother is, commonly, the nurturer of the child and serves more as the pillar of support for emotional growth and comfort.

The role of the father is important for strength and stability. When the father is also involved in the day to day care of the child such as dressing, feeding and in other roles even as the child grows older, it offers comfort and help in strengthening the child character. It is in the best interest of a child to be raised by both parents in a peaceful and loving environment. Child rearing does not just run through the period of infancy to adulthood, it is usually a life time process because parents continue to get involved in the lives of their adult children at one point or another, especially in spiritual and advisory capacity.

A lot of responsibilities go with parenting and we need the help of God in applying biblical principles in raising our children the bible way. How you rear your children is different from stage to stage but what should remain constant is your trust and reliance on the finished work of Jesus Christ.

Preparation for Parenthood

Parenting takes time, effort and maturity. Preparation time is never wasted. Proper preparation will always save you a lot of headaches, money and time in the long run. Someone once said that if you start preparing after the arrival of the baby, you are a little late. Preparation must be started much earlier, and it is important to prepare yourself psychologically, emotionally and even financially. Get yourself ready to be involved in every aspect of the child's life. It involves spending yourself, time and money. This is because you are embarking on a journey that takes a child to a mature adult. This is not just the change in the physical body but also in character and strength. So it is important to start preparing well before the children arrive as it will contribute immensely to your success as a parent. You do this by building up yourself–working hard, saving money and educating yourself. Also, build up your backbone physically and spiritually. Cultivate the habit of listening to God and following His instructions. You want to be able to "make" your children "real" sons and daughters by way of solid training and pouring yourself into their lives. They will thank you for it in the future and would hold you in high esteem. You too will be filled with a great sense of achievement and gratifications. God himself will honor and reward you.

The importance of properly raising and training a child cannot be overemphasized. Giving birth to a child is just the beginning; you have just brought a child to the world, such a child needs to be shown the world. The child needs to be socially guided and be shown the way around, and through the world. Unfortunately some biological parents are not available to do this and others will have to step up to the plate.

Naming a Child

What is in a Name? Names carry a lot of weights and meanings in the life of an individual. In the bible culture, the names have meaning and reasons; some names describe the personality of the individuals that bear the names. Whatever you want to name your child, make sure you research the meaning and know that it is something good. A word of caution though, just because you find a name in the bible does not mean that it is good. For example, I know a couple of names that mean "sorrow" in the bible. I do not want to name my child sorrow, I don't think anybody should. If there is any unpleasant story related to the child, God can always turn every sorrow into joy. Teach the children themselves to avoid calling themselves bad names, if they have to pick a nickname or you as the parent are picking for them, make sure it's something good and uplifting.

Be sure you know the reason behind a name before you give it to your child. He will probably answer to this name for the rest of his life, and can begin to act the meaning of this name, too many bad examples around. So make sure the name has a good meaning, not just something for the purpose of a name. God himself had to change Abram to Abraham, Sarai to Sarah, and Jacob to Israel. Answering to negative names and nicknames can come to limit such individuals and be fulfilled in such life.

Making a Monster or a Responsible Adult

The word "make" is a process. Think in terms of baking a cake, you have your ingredients with flour as the major item; you mix it with egg, water, butter and others. You keep mixing until smooth and then put it in the oven. The expected outcome is a cake. It takes a lot of different input at different stages to come up with the cake including the application of heat that brings about the golden color, the aroma and the delicious sweet taste.

In the same manner, when you train your child, you engage in the process of "making" the child a responsible adult who will do you proud in the future. Leave the child untrained or overprotected, you would have just created a monster that will become a menace to you and the society at large. You should get to work as soon as the child arrives. How do you work on a New born? The bible says if the foundation be destroyed what can the righteous do? Ps.11:3.

The newly arrived requires a lot of caring more than training but I also like to submit to you that you have plenty of room for training already, even at that early stage. For example, the newborn enjoys the warm hands of the parents and because the baby is the bundle of joy now and the center of the whole world at this stage, everybody loves and wants to carry him or her. Before you knew what was happening, the baby gets used to the hand and cries when you put him or her in the crib or the bed. You don't want to hear the cry; it gets you nervous or emotional and wants to make you cry too. What do you do you? Carry the baby again and the cycle continues. You should train the baby to sleep in the crib or the bed, and a little cry will not harm him/her. In fact some said it is good for the lungs. You cannot keep carrying the baby in your arms as you need to be able to move around to do something else like returning to work.

Another example is that when they are that young they cry from every little discomfort primarily because they cannot really communicate verbally. When they cry, the first thing most parents do is rush food into their mouth. They are not necessarily hungry when they cry. There are many other reasons why the baby may cry. Do a little investigation to find out the correct reason for the cry. You may need to do a couple of things, like changing the position, checking the diaper to see if it's wet and needs changing. The baby's temperature is almost the same as that of an adult, if you feel too warm or too cold in an environment, the baby is probably feeling the same and would cry. Don't overdress the baby. Lastly check the last time the baby was fed; he/she may truly be hungry. If you keep pushing the feeding bottle or the breast at the first sign of discomfort (crying), you may be sending a wrong message. It is possible that babies nurtured this way may grow up reaching for food for comfort at the first sign or symptom of stress and discomfort. This can lead to overeating causing uncontrolled weight problem. You can be sure in this life everyone will experience stress at one time or another. If you feel that the cry is not normal or unusual, like high pitch tone, crying incessantly, seek help. Take the baby to the Doctor.

As the baby continues to grow, remember to make routine appointment with the pediatrician for the monitoring of the child's growth and development at each milestone. As the baby is being cared for physically daily and routinely monitored by the doctor, you engage in daily prayer, speaking the word of God over the baby's life.

Tantrums

As the child continues to develop and grow to become a toddler, you may notice tantrums. It is an emotional outburst mostly seen in kids and sometimes in people with emotional distress. This could be overcome, but if not handled the right way it may turn to a big problem that may continue in the adult life. As previously mentioned, commit the child to the hand of God even at this stage as in any other stage. Do not accept the conventional way of calling him/her the terrible "two". Your child is not terrible and you are doing all you can now to "make" him/her an awesome child. You may start to notice tantrum around the age of two. It happens when a child is frustrated over a situation, sometimes simply not being able to express himself/herself properly or inability to make needs known. This can lead to excessive crying, stubbornness, screaming, and being un-consolable. Parent of toddler are expected to help guide and teach the child and establish basic routines such as hand washing, brushing teeth and others. It is also normal for toddlers to be frequently frustrated. It is an essential step to their development. They-will learn through experience, trial and error. When frustrated, they often behave "badly" with actions like screaming, hitting or biting. Parent should be careful when reacting to such behavior. Giving threat or punishment is not helpful and will only make situation worse, and lead to temper tantrum. Temper tantrum could be manipulative or born out of frustration.

Manipulative tantrum: Toddlers know how to push mothers' button using tantrum to get his/her way. Be firm if you find out that your child is doing this. They are young but they know you. If you are volatile it will be easy for such child to trigger an explosion from you ending in a screaming match with no winner.

Frustration tantrum: Many time this is from a child's inability to properly express himself or herself, as quick as the motor skills and mental skills are functioning. In this case communication is imperative. Be patient with the child. Offer help; come to his/ her level.

In all cases, be prayerful and declare the peace of our Lord Jesus Christ on the child daily.

Home Environment

Providing a conducive and a pleasant home environment is very helpful. The home environment should be clean and tidy, safe, joyful, comfortable, conducive, and free of strife, at all time. In the bible story popularly known as the parable of the prodigal son (Luke 15:11-32), the so called prodigal son still found it within his heart to return home. He did not say "I would rather die, or, join the gang," and then his life would have gone into a downward spiral from that moment. He did not say "if my father sees me, he will tear me apart." He remembered home, he remembered it was a better place than the pigs' pen where he was; he must have remembered getting love and support at home. Parents should make their home a place where love thrives, where the children will like to return to, from time to time, even when they are already grown and become independent.

Love and Support

Children should be raised in love and abundance of it too. Let them know that they are loved by God and you. Jesus was tempted shortly after public announcement that he was loved by God (Matt. 3:17-Matt. 4:1-3). They will most likely overcome temptation when they know they are loved by God and equally by their parents. Isaiah 43... you are precious and honored. Remind and show them that they are loved by God and the family. Emphasize the love of God. Let them know that they are loved by their family and much more by God. Showing them love helps to prevent poor self esteem.

Show love, teach love, allow children to learn from your example. Love gives, love shares, love sacrifices. It is not always convenient; love does what it takes. They should remember to love themselves too; they have some responsibilities towards self in order for life to continue. Showing your child how much you love him/her or hearing it from the parent empowers them to go out there and face life. It gives them some level of strength.

If there is a problem outside, let them know they can always count on your support. Let them know they can come to you for refuge, while you sort things out. If what they did was wrong, as you point it out to them, let them know that in God there is always a way out. He is the one that makes a way where there is no way. Example: The prodigal son, as previously mentioned knows to return home again.

Rule with Love

When you love a child, and show it even when it comes to time to discipline, he will understand. Let him know that no matter what, he will always be your child and you will always love him.

Spending Time

Spend time as much as possible; the more time, the better. It is an expression of your love. Suggested Reading – "To every child, LOVE is spelled T-I-M-E. Avoid spending your time working too hard at multiple jobs away from them, just to provide materials for them.

The time to relate with children must not be sacrificed for work to get "more stuff." It is alright to work to provide for children but doing it in excess is often counterproductive. You should endeavor to maintain a balance. Otherwise, you get blamed by the same child/children when they grow up and recognize what went missing in their lives as due parental absenteeism.

The children understand when you spend time with them as an expression of your love. There are cases where the parents need to work harder even to meet the minimal basic needs. Such parents still need to make conscious effort to make out quality time for children no matter how small. You may plan to do activities together, e.g.

eating, praying (Family Prayer time), and doing household chores.

Do your best and allow God to help you set your priority right. The race is not for the swift neither the battle for the strong. Eccl.9:11. Some trust in chariots and some in horses but we will remember the Name of our Lord. Psalm 20:7

Values Vs Materials

Some parents think they must work more to provide for their children what they (parents) did not have when they were young. As you provide them with what you the parent did not have as a child, make sure you also provide them with what you have. Provide them with the values that will enable them to grow up successfully as responsible adult. You can only do this by spending time with them. They will thank you for it in the future. It will give you a sense of fulfillment to see your children, grow up to become great men and women who are strong in character and virtues and going places. What a mental rest you will enjoy. If your goal is only to work hard and provide material wealth for them, they will take the materials and still turn against you or if care is not taken; without proper upbringing, the material provision could become a snare to them, and you may have yourself to blame.

Spending time with them does not indicate softness as some people will like to point out. It helps you to know them better and relate with them in unique ways. Again, it is an expression of your love for them. Stay in touch, even when they are grown and are no longer with you, for example when they are gone off to college. If there is a need for discipline due to misbehavior or an offence, do not hesitate but do so in love, and continue in your relationship. Teach them how to take responsibility for their actions, and teach them how to forgive.

Forgiveness

Be ready to forgive; do it without grudge and without reservation. Do not keep referring to the same issue over and over even after they have apologized or have even been disciplined for the same issue. If you wronged your children, it is okay to ask them for forgiveness also.

See the example of the parable of the lost son popularly known as the prodigal son. Luke 15:11-32. By any human standard what the son did was terrible. It was like telling the father that since you have refused to die early enough, just give me my portion of your wealth (my inheritance) and I will be out of your way, and you can decide to live forever. He took the wealth and left with no intention of returning home.

See what happened to him. If we analyze this deeper, this son came back not out of genuine repentance but because he was hungry and he thought he would die of hunger. When there was nowhere else to turn to, he remembered home. But, look at the love of a father; he did not hold the sin against the son. He ran out to meet with the son and even celebrated his return by throwing a big party. This father is a picture of our heavenly father, and he should be our model. Our heavenly father loves us unconditionally and is ever willing to forgive us completely without reservation whenever we return to Him. "Can't Nobody do us like Jesus". No wonder David said I would rather fall into the hand of God than the hand of men.

Example of King David and his son, Absalom:

King David missed the relationship with his son Absalom who had left home after killing his half-brother. We can see that what Absalom did was terrible. He committed murder and took justice into his hand. Absalom fled home, but his father, the king still loved him and secretly longed to reconcile with Absalom (2 Samuel 13:39). Absalom was later allowed to return home but never into the king's presence for at least the first two years. Later he demanded to see the king; he came to the presence of the king and bowed his face to the earth. The king kissed him without saying a word: Proverbs 27:5 "better is an open rebuke than a secret love". This led to a greater problem that cost Absalom his life and even the nation dearly.

Teach children not to burn the bridge to the home. "You already grew up with so many years of relationship that has become part of you. Some can't wait to get out of the house. There would be a part of you that would long for the home (your root) no matter how successful you become. Do your best to not destroy the relationship". Children need to forgive when the case demands and ask for forgiveness if they make mistakes or offend other family members or anybody at all.

Absalom showed up essentially to seek a full pardon but showed no sign of repentance by his statement, even though he bowed down with his face to the ground (1Sam.14:32). No wonder he later led a rebellion against his father and his kingdom, and he died, plunging the nation into a war and all its consequences. All these could have been avoided. The father, king David still loved him (Absalom) and wanted to forgive but he did not express it.

Control

This could be positive (healthy) or negative (unhealthy)

Control could be positive as in setting limits, training and discipline. It becomes negative when it becomes a means by which the child or parent manipulates one another. This could be both ways with the parents controlling child or the child controlling parents.

Child-to Parent:

Normally the child should not control the parents, and if it happens, it is a problem. Usually, a child senses an area of weakness in the parent and takes advantage of that to get his/her way. For example, if the parent gets excessively nervous when the child is sick, he or she can start faking illness or exaggerate an existing condition so that the parent could give in to his/her demand. We all have soft spots, but we should not allow it to become a button that the child would be pushing to get his/her ways because it may be dangerous.

Parent-to Child:

Avoid use of fear, threat and manipulation in controlling a child. It is only a matter of time before the child finds out the truth and the child would hate the parent or at least the parent loses his/her respect. If you use fear and threat in getting them to do what you want. It may translate to manipulation and the bible equates that with witchcraft. They would find out the truth later and you lose their respect. Do not use fear and threat even in seemingly harmless or playful way. e.g. The boogeyman is coming to get you, if you go out he will attack or "the cop is coming to get you". You are the parent, you have such a strong influence, and they believe what you say. There have been instances in which the children grew up but are still being influenced by the fear instilled into them at that tender age. Pass your point across in a simple harmless way. Let them know you can help them do what they want at the appropriate time and manner. Do not sow the seed of fear and horror through the movies either. The child will soon find out it is an empty threat and will no longer obey you.. Explain what you want at the child's level and encourage simple obedience. Abstain from the use of any form of manipulation, magic, illusion etc. The bible calls them witchcraft. It is mind control. You do this just to control the child or keep him/her in check. Keeping the child in check without manipulation is possible especially when both parents are involved.

Single parent can also do a good job, that brings us to single parenthood.

Single Parenting

Do not set out to be a single parent. God has a good reason for wanting two parents to raise a child. Things can happen along the way, such as loss of one parent or separation. So where there is a single parent, trust God to be the other parent and He will surely help you, and the child will turn out great. The common thing is that the child is left with the mother to be the single parent. Such mothers should allow the participation of the father where possible. Fatherhood is so important in the lives of the children so much that some people call it a special anointing.

Fatherhood

Prov.17:6

Father needs to be involved with their children. The importance of fathers engaging in the care of the children cannot be overemphasized. Statistics have shown that children without active fathers in their lives are more prone to having problems than the ones with the fathers. The following is a disturbing statistics from the Centers of Disease Control and Prevention (CDC), Interagency Forum of Child and Family, Criminal Justice and behavior: 63 percent of youth suicides happen in fatherless homes

90 percent of homeless runaway teenagers are from fatherless homes

85 percent of children who have behavioral problems come from fatherless homes

71 percent of High School dropouts come from fatherless homes

75 percent of teenagers in jail cells are from fatherless homes

77 percent teen & kids in rehabilitation facilities are from fatherless homes

85 percent of rapist are from homes in which the fathers are not involved

Almost 50% of children born today are born into fatherless

Fatherless children are twice likely to drop out of schools than those classmates with two parents. 72 percent of all teenage murderers grew up without fathers

Fatherless children are 11 times more likely to exhibit violent behaviors than children with two parents in a home.

80 percent of adolescent in psych hospitals are from fatherless homes

70 percent of kids incarcerated right now came from fatherless homes

3 out of 4 suicides are happening in fatherless homes

Girls who are raised in fatherless homes are 164 percent more likely to get pregnant before marriage. 92 percent more likely to get a divorce if married

The absence of biological fathers increases by 900 percent a daughter's vulnerability to be raped and sexually abused because most of them happen by boyfriends or stepfathers of custodial mothers.

Children in fatherless homes consistently score lower in math & reading

The greatest predictability of criminal behavior is the absence of a father in the home

The above noted statistical finding is just a part of much more findings. Mere reading through, speaks volume about the impact of the participation of the fathers in the lives of their children. It is therefore important for fathers that are not in the homes to maintain contacts with their children.

If you are a single mother, you have the job of combining the role of the father with your role as the mother. You have a daunting task at hand. The Lord can help. He can be a true father to your children and help you in raising them. Jesus is the father of the fatherless Ps. 68:5. If it is at all possible allow the participation of the father in the care of the child, at least for the sake of the child. Where it is not possible, trust God, believe in Him.

You may also look into getting some men as father figure in their lives, as mentor, guide etc. But please be very careful. Do this prayerfully. Do not be naïve; do not open up your child for physical, sexual and psychological abuse. God Himself will help you; there is nothing too hard for Him to do. If fatherlessness is due to a failed marriage and mother decides to remarry, do not force the new husband as father of kids especially when they are already grown. If possible do not sever their relationship with their father. If they already know their father, do not force a different father on them. It is ok to maintain the relationship with their father or at least keep in touch and then develop this new relationship gradually.

King Solomon and his father King David is a perfect biblical example of the importance of the father's involvement in the life of a child. Read the book of 1king 3, Prov. 1:4 and Ps.72. King Solomon was able to ask God for wisdom when he was prompted to ask for what he wanted. 1 King 3:1-5, 2 chronicles 1 based on the teachings of the father.

What you **leave in them** is much more important than what you **leave for them**. With an estimated wealth of over 200 billion of today's value, King Solomon was not only the richest in the Old Testament but also the richest king now, going by the current value of his wealth then. After offering unusual sacrifice to the LORD, God appeared to him and allowed him to ask for whatever he wanted. He did not ask for riches, but for wisdom, knowledge and understanding. God decided to give him riches in addition to his request. We would notice in Proverbs 4 that King Solomon gave the credit to his father who taught him, among other things, that "wisdom is the principal thing…and with all your getting, get understanding" Having been schooled in the school of wisdom, he did not fail to ask for wisdom when the opportunity arose. He asked for wisdom, knowledge and understanding. Solomon had a deep grasp of how the three are related and how they work together. We can find the proof all through the book of Proverbs and other bible books credited to Solomon, as the author. Thousands of years later, we are still talking about Solomon's wealth. Again the role of fathers in the lives of their children cannot be over estimated. Fathers need to be present and active.

Fathers therefore should be very much part of the job of raising children. Fathers that are present in the lives of the children should really be present meaning to be actively involved in the lives of their children. Some fathers are available yet they act like absentee father; they are present, but not there e.g. Always working, spending no time with family and particularly the children. When they are available they are reading newspapers, watching their favorite sport television channels etc. Children cannot talk to them. This should not happen.

Where the two parents are not together, the visiting parent (mostly the father) should not talk ill about the other parent to the children, even when it is true. You may not praise unbecoming attitude, but watch how you talk to them about their mother/father.

Anger

Where both parents are involved in the upbringing, avoid anger and conflicts. Children are terrified of this kind of emotion around them. They feel insecure, they don't know what to expect. Learn to stay calm especially in times of pressure or turmoil. You will make better choices if you do. Plus it is a virtue that is noticeable to everyone if you are calm under pressure when others are not. Anyone could be of his or her best behavior when the going is good. The true test of your character is being able to stay cool in the face of chaos or problems.

Control your anger. Anger rests in the bosom of fools (Eccl.7:9). As you control your anger, your children learn by example, and you can morally teach them anger control. If you find yourself in anger too often, you may want to sit back, tune in and check the cause of your anger. Oftentimes it is from a different reason, probably some unresolved conflict. Seek help if needed. Go to God in prayer. It is always helpful. If it's due to past failure, get rid of the guilt and condemnation by trusting Jesus. Release it into His hands as the forgiver of sins, He will take the feelings away and restore you. He will put courage and strength in your heart and take away guilt and shame.

Other People Raising Children for you

Ask yourself some pertinent questions: are the values of these other people the same as yours? Is this how you want your child to be raised? Choose positively and in wisdom. Timothy's grandmother in the bible is a perfect example of how impactful other people can be. (2Tim 1:5)

Think about the implication and make your choice wisely because children can easily get into terrible habit or behavior that you may not ordinarily condone. Such other people could be Grandmother, Family Member, friends/Neighbors

Television

Don't surrender your child to television. Don't allow the television to raise your children for you. Of course don't say no, all the time. Ask God for wisdom. You can use several approaches. Personally, when my kids were young, we were able to prevail on them not to watch televisions during weekdays because of homework and other reading they had to do. They watched television on weekends and on Sundays, Christian tv and later sports included. When they were much younger they watched public television, children's television that we were comfortable with. Whatever program they are going to be watching regularly, take time to watch it with them occasionally; know what it's all about. Make sure it is not something that contradicts your beliefs and values. As you watch the show with them, especially movies and dramas, if there is a scene that does not line up with what you believe in, make the correction right away. Mention the good and acceptable part, and mention the bad part. Tell them what is wrong with it, and if possible, if they are confronted with such, what they can do about it.

School

Do not abandon your child to school for training. Train your child, of course they are going to learn a lot from school, it will not be enough. By the time they enter school there must be some level of structure in them. Prepare them for school, teach them to know some of their numbers and alphabets before entering school so that they don't feel out of place when they encounter other children who are already solid by the time they start school. This help them to fit in rather than acting like a spoiled brat which can set them up for failure not just in school but in life also. The Bible says if the foundation be destroyed, What can the righteous do?

Freedom/Independence

It is not always possible to follow them around, doing that can send a wrong signal and push them. If you have truly done a good job in raising them you can be rest assured that they will do the right thing. The bible says "my children shall be taught of the Lord and great shall be the peace of my children" Isaiah 54:13. Meditate on this scripture or similar ones often, concerning them, and believe it with all your heart, the Lord Himself will direct them and they will be sensitive to the leading of the Holy Spirit. Release them into the hand of God; commit them into His hands prayerfully. You can always live confidently in faith knowing and believing the scripture "for I know whom I have believed and I am fully persuaded that He is able to keep that which I have committed to His hands 2 Tim.1:12. If you have truly yielded and committed them to His hands, He is truly more than able. Just rest in His love, for you and your children.

Being Observant

As much as you want them to be free, you must be observant. If you see signs and symptoms of rebelliousness, affirm the blessings in the finished work of Jesus, and declare that they are signs and wonder. Isaiah 8:18... Behold, I and the children whom the Lord had given me are for signs and for wonders in Israel from the Lord of hosts which dwells in mount Zion. Let them get born again as early as they can. Introduce the new birth concept and who they are in Jesus and keep affirming their righteousness in Christ Jesus, even in the face of negative signs and symptoms. Psalms 23:5, thou prepare a table before me in the presence of my enemies. Keep choosing your words, talking about who you want them to be, not what you don't like in them.

Observe for good signs and for bad signs also. Parents should be observant; when we see something unique or different, we should help to nurture, guide and develop it. Jochebed, the mother of Moses, saw that Moses was a "beautiful" child and defied the order of the king, Exodus 2. Observe for change in behavior, the language they speak, including use of words and profanity. You are the prophet of your own life, and "death and life are in the power of the tongues and they that love it shall eat the fruit thereof." Proverbs 18:21. Thou art snared with the words of thy mouth, thou art taken with the word of thy mouth. Proverb 6:2. "For by your words you will be justified, and by your words you will be condemned". Matt. 12:37. Watch what you say to them and what they say to themselves. This starts with the name you give to them

Profanity and Negative Words

Words are powerful. They should be taught to watch what they say about themselves. Esau sold his birthright with his own words. It was meant to be a joke…Genesis 25:29-end.but it later haunted him. Another example was a co-worker that used to joke around, calling his fiancée his "future ex-wife." I was never comfortable around him with such a joke. Occasionally I would tell him to stop talking like that. The courtship lasted one year and they got married. One year later the marriage ended. Never allow your ear to hear your mouth predict your defeat. Stress or emphasize the positive use of speech. As parents avoid using words to demean and diminish children.

Jacob complained that his life was full of woes Genesis 48:9. He died much younger than his predecessors. Use your words positively on them; teach them to use words positively on themselves. Don't allow them to use negative words or profanity. They may want to tell you "it's okay, it's just a saying." Col. 4:6 says let your conversation be always full of grace and seasoned with salt. Ephesians 4:29 says do not let any unwholesome thought come out of your mouth. Let them know it may be acceptable within some subcultures but they should know they belong to the heavenly culture, where corrupt communication is not permitted to proceed out of their mouths (Ephesians 4:29).

Sherry Ronke

Talking down/Nagging

Avoid nagging. If they did something wrong, correct, discipline, move on and let it be over. Don't keep referring to it. When you find yourself as a parent, nagging and scolding excessively, you may want to stop and look inward. There may be an underlying issue that is probably not related to the child that you need to deal with, instead of displacing it on the children. Don't make them an easy target or prey. Do not talk down to them, it destroys self-esteem. They believe you when you tell them they are fat, they are ugly, Avoid rudeness in your words and communication. Teach them to be respectful and courteous.

Respect

In this area parent also need to live by example. Both parents should respect each other in the presence of their children. They should avoid running each other down even when they have problems with each other or cannot get along. In so doing, children will learn to respect not only both parents but also others and even their spouses when the time comes. Fathers should show love to mothers at least in the presence of the children. I once heard that the greatest gift a father can give to his children is to love their mother. Maintain a joyful environment, children learns the most in such environment.

Honor

It is an internal attitude, respect and courtesy. It also means high respect for worth, merit or rank. When applied to God, it means to worship God, or to reverence Him. It also means to show courteous regard. Teach your child to honor self and others—parents, elders, including people in authority. As a parent, honor your own parents. Teach your children to honor and respect you. It is the law of the Lord. Matt 15:5-8, Deut.27:6. Children who mock their parents, ravens will pluck out the eyes (loss of vision and direction, in complete darkness about life and the way to go). Proverbs 30:17. In the same manner they have to learn to relate with God with heartfelt honor and reverence, including other people in authority over them. Isaiah 29:!3. The bible teaches emphatically that we must give honor to whom honor is due. Romans 13:7

Courtesy

It is a gentle, polite, and courtly manner, a behavior marked by polished manners or respect for others. How do you respect yourself and others? Keep your word and promises, avoid being loud and noisy. Avoid rudeness. Keep yourself clean, neat and tidy, not making others uncomfortable. Using of cell phones so loud in the public, cutting into people while talking can be considered rudeness.

Etiquette

Avoid loud jokes, poking nose, picking teeth in the public, using dental floss in the public, blowing nose, spitting, belching, farting, not washing hands, talking with food in your mouth. Etiquette is different from place to place, the list can continue.

Misbehaving

If this is becoming a problem, employ the use of prayer. Declare what you want to see and not what you are seeing. In the school of faith "believing is seeing" not vice versa as popularly known. The bible teaches us to call those things that be not as though they were. You see manifestation of faith as an invisible coin; believing and speaking are the two sides of this coin. You believe God to change the behavior of the child and you keep declaring that this child is a great child with perfect and acceptable behavior and soon you will begin to see the manifestation of your declaration.

If the misbehavior is just starting, be sensitive and quick enough to notice and start redirecting and retraining as soon as possible. If the child has never been trained or habilitated in the first place, you cannot retrain or rehabilitate. You just have to start the training or habilitation at that point of notice. It is better to be late than never.

If temper tantrum is a problem, parent themselves should avoid throwing tantrum. Also parent should understand when the child is using tantrum as a means of control. If child is misbehaving outside if you have never corrected such manner of behavior at home don't start correcting this behavior outside or at least use wisdom. It sends wrong signal and confusion.

Physical Appearance/Dressing

Teach your children to be comfortable with their own body and not to allow others to dictate how they should look. Ps.139:14. They are fearfully and wonderfully made. TV should not be their standard of physique and appearance. Teach them to look unto Jesus. He is beautiful. Jesus is the fairest of 10,000, Song of Solomon 5:10. He is altogether lovely, we are like him. In the bible the songs of Solomon depicts the loving beauty of our Lord and Savior. It is a wonderful privilege to look like him. If they are overweight don't treat as a stigma, work on reducing weight slowly, nothing drastic. Let them see the doctor, something could be wrong with their rate of metabolism or there may be other underlying problem. They should avoid overeating if they are indulging in that. I was watching a television talk show in which the mother of a teenager was saying that her daughter was "fat". She said that her daughter must lose her weight at all cost. She even said if the girl did not submit to stomach bypass surgery that she would "yank" the fat out of her daughter's body. The girl was overweight, but it was not like she weighs 350lbs. Mother is probably size 4 while the daughter who would be between 14-16yrs of age is probably size 16. I guess she wants the daughter to be her (mother) size. I believe she can pass her message across to her daughter differently and not to be so forceful and derogatory about it.

Teach modesty. Be good examples. Sometimes parents want to dress kids up. Remember they are not your "dolls". Do not make them your dolls. We want to dress them up; we have our dreams and ideas of what we want them to look like. They have the minds of their own. Allow them to choose, as long as value and decency are not compromised. Remind them the primary reasons for dressings are protection, safety and decency; fashion is secondary. You must take the weather and the environment into consideration in your choice. Learn that your clothings and attire should not define you. Avoid falling into the trap of "must be in the vogue" kind of wear – designer. Many designers are nice and beautiful but could be very expensive too. Wearing them should not be a do or die affair for you.

Same thing goes for shoes, accessories, hairstyle, and tattoo. Beware of what you put on yourself as some of them have gang and cult undertone. Be sure you understand what the material you are putting on yourself stand for before you wear them. A young man was killed because he was mistaken for a rivalry gang member due to the fact that he was wearing a red bandana that looks like a gang member sign. The rivalry gang gunned him down and they later found out it was an error. This young man had a promising future that was cut short. It was a loss to the family and the society at large.

Hygiene/health maintenance

They are practices that help to promote and preserve health. Daily make it a part of you. Teach to children. Practice it yourself and live by example.

Food/eating

Eat nutritious meal. Avoid empty calories that never nourish your body. Limit consumption of food with high level of High fructose corn syrup. It is proven to kill your appetite and makes you want to eat frequently, leading to weight gain. A lot of children are overweight and it is becoming an epidemic. Parents have a role to play in making sure children maintain healthy weight. Most diseases are associated with excess weight directly or indirectly. Engage in physical exercises avoid getting into crash diet programs; that could be dangerous.

Exercise

Children should be encouraged to engage in activities that allow them to move their body more. Bodily exercise profits little(1 Timothy 4:18).The bible confirms that there are some level of advantages in physical exercise. Avoid or engage less in inactive program like digital games and TV. Interact with real people.

Other helpful tools for Parenting.
Prayer (see Chapter 5)
Reading

Encourage reading. Somebody once said, "what exercise is to the physical body is what reading is to the brain". It helps in expanding and enlarging one's thinking capacity. Be a reader yourself and share your experience with the children. You may have reading projects together. May be a book of the bible or other inspirational books that can also help in molding their characters.

Suggested Readings:

The Bible

There is a Spirit behind every word spoken by God; the Spirit of God himself. He said in the book of John 6:63 that the word that I speak to you, they are spirit and they are life. cultivate the habit of reading the bible. Let it become a part of you. The Psalmist says thy word is a lamp to my feet and the light onto my path. Psalm 119:105. Apostle Paul said "How can we escape if we neglect such a great salvation which at first was spoken by the Lord. Heb. 2:3. The bible is the spoken word of the lord, as we read and study it, and open our hearts to the Holy Spirit, we receive more and more from the Lord.

Biography

This is the life story of an individual. We can be inspired by what motivate other people to succeed, and learn from how they overcame challenges.

Inspirational

We can be inspired and even inspire others by reading inspirational stories, fictions and non fictions alike.

Gratitude

This is the quality of being thankful, readiness to show appreciation for, and return kindness. It is the feelings of being grateful. Teach children gratitude. You as a parent must live a lifestyle of gratitude so that you will be a good example. Even when it is their right to receive something, they must show appreciation for it. The only thing that we can give to God is our praise and gratitude. Teach them to appreciate you as parents. Appreciate them as well. Praise them for good deeds no matter how small and negligible. Your praise and admiration must be genuine. They can sense it when you are pretending, we are all intuitive. Avoid murmuring and complaining.

Teenagers and the adolescent stage of life.

The children need the care of the parent at every stage of life. During the teenage years, parent should not fall into the trap of thinking that children are mature and they can take good care of themselves. This is true in many areas but not so true is some other areas. At this stage, they need to be monitored more closely and be kept under close supervision or observation. There is a delicate balance between doing this correctly and doing it excessively. You cannot suspect every move they make and start provoking them. The bible warns us to not provoke our children. Ephesians 6:4, Colossians 3:21. At this stage of life, a lot of hormonal changes is happening to their body and this will bring about physical changes and psychological changes as well as behavioral changes. They need the parental support and explanation of these changes. Encourage them to ask questions and answer the questions as honest as possible. Remember they can easily ask these questions somewhere else and be given wrong answers and responses that are not appropriate. As parent you cannot be with them 24 hours, the more reason to lean more on Jesus and be sensitive in your spirit.

Physical changes

There is an enormous change in the physical body of both male and female during this period. The change is very rapid, the voice may be cracking. Some will think they are sick. It is the job of the parent to explain this phase to their teenager. Parent need to be well educated in these changes. Puberty which is a state of sexual awakening happens in this stage. The sexual organs and the reproductive system of the child begin to develop. There is breast development, hair growth in armpit and pubic areas. The female starts menstruation and the male experiences wet dreams. They need to understand that any sexual intercourse during this period may lead to unwanted pregnancy. They need to be told point and clear, not in idioms.

Psychological and behavioral changes

Mood swings is common due to hormonal changes. There is a desire to be with friends and much more for opposite sex. They might even think of marriage and lifelong partners. At this stage it is important for them to grasp the importance of being able to tell the difference between love, lust and infatuation. They need to slow than in their decision making and allow the guidance of the Holy Spirit. The increased desire for relationships among age groups and classmates causes increased need for acceptance among peers. This may lead to something called peer Pressure.

Peer Pressure

This is influence extorted by a peer group, encouraging individuals to change their attitude, values, or behaviors in order to conform to group norms. The changes that happens to the adolescents leads to increase need for acceptance. Children at this stage may experience a fear of being disliked, fear of being laughed at. They may feel the need to be accepted at all cost and so may begin to conform, many times to bad ways and habits. They could be told having sex is cool and the thing in vogue. The bible calls sexual intercourse outside marriage a sin. They should be instructed to stay strong when under pressure. This is a good stage to meditate on the love of God. Jesus loves you no matter what. He is the friend that sticks closer than a brother. He is altogether lovely. You have Jesus You have it all. Dare to be different; you are building yourself as and sons and daughters of God. Have a good self esteem. Don't sell yourself cheap. Do not underestimate yourself. Know who you are. Children must be taught to learn to delay gratification. This is delayed enjoyment or pleasure till later when it is more appropriate.

Other Ways to help Children to overcome Peer Pressure:

Teach the revelation love of God
Show love and acceptance
Maintain peace at home
Prayer and the word of God

- Psalms 63:3 your loving kindness is better than life-make that your watchword. The loving kindness of Jesus, which is better than life is much better than that peer trying to push you to do something that is not proper. You do not need to seek the acceptance of peer that would push you to do evil. You are already accepted by Jesus in the beloved. Eph.1:6
- Open Communication; the more communication that takes place, the more likely your teens are

going to tell you what is happening in their life. Don't be suspicious and start questioning every of their move. You will drive them away.

- Listen.-Don't jump to conclusions
- Don't make mountains of molehills
- Don't be too rigid if safety and values are not compromised
- Look for cue. Pay attention to change in behavior, withdrawing, drop in grades, skipping school, breaking rules
- Love Unconditionally. Show them you love them no matter what.
- Share time together (see the book for every child love is spell T-I-M-E).When you spend time together your family strength is manifested in a unique way that helps your child resist outer negative influence better.
- Remember as Jesus is so are you. John 1:16, we have the mind of Christ, because of the born again experience we are joint heirs with Jesus. One spirit with Him, sealed with the Holy Spirit.

How to handle the stage of adolescence

Children need the comfort and the reassurance of their parents. Parents should answer their questions as honestly as possible, and don't push them around. Something like the child coming to the mother to ask a question and she said "I don't know, go and ask your father". He or she goes to the father who mirrors the previous answer and said to the child, "I don't know go and ask your mom. You can be sure such child will get his or her answer but may be from a wrong source with a wrong perspective. He or she will no longer go the parents.

Parents must do their best to supply the need of the children. Provide necessary support, be available. Let them know that they can always count on you. this is the time to stress on relationship with the Holy Spirit. Get on this yourself as a parent, get materials that you can study together and make it a way of life.

Chapter 3

Training

Training means to bring a person to an agreed standard of proficiency. A synonym is "habilitate" (where we get the word, "rehabilitation" from), means to impart an ability or capacity. If a child has never been habilitated, trained or instructed, such will be very difficult to rehabilitate when derailed. They have to start with habilitation which is real training. A child left to himself brings shame to his mother. Prov. 29:15. I always wonder why the bible, in this scripture passage, points to the mother. I seriously believe is not just the mother, but the father also and even the society at large.

I once read about a study purportedly conducted about two popular families; Max Jukes and Jonathan Edwards, in the 19th and 20th century. Max Jukes was an atheist who got married to a godless woman. The summary of the legacy of this family is of extreme criminality, poverty and diseases. Some 560 descendants of this family were traced. 310 died as paupers, 150 became criminals, in prison at one point or another. 7 of them were murderers, 100 were known to be drunkards and more than half of the women were prostitutes. The descendants of Max Jukes cost the state more than $1.3millions in 19th Century dollars which is much more than that in today's value. This is a sad story, what a posterity?

On the other hand is the story of Jonathan Edwards Family who was said to be a contemporary of Max Jukes. He was a committed Christian who was married to a godly woman. Some 1,394 descendants were traced. 295 graduated from college of whom 13 became college presidents and 65 became professors, 3 were elected as United States senators, 3 were state governors and others were sent as ministers to foreign countries, 30 were judges, 100 were lawyers, 56 were physicians, 75 were officers in the military, 100 were well known missionaries, preachers and prominent authors, another 80 held some form of public office of whom there were mayors of large cities. One was the Comptroller of the U.S Treasury and another was the vice president of the United States. The Bible says "…...The generation of the upright shall be blessed." Psalm 112:2

Looking at above two families, it will be noted that it is important to take the job of raising children seriously. Successful child training takes commitment, determination and trust in God. The bible says "correct your son, he will give you rest" Prov. 29:17. It is not enough just to bring children to the world we must show them the world also. Train them and make sure they do not become a burden to the society.

When should training start? As early as possible, the bible says "train up a child when young, when he grows old, he will not depart." (Proverbs 1:8, Proverbs 3:1-2). Some of the elements of training were discussed in the chapter on Parenting, and more will be discussed in the following pages. Proverbs 29:17 Correction of a child brings delight and desire.

Responsibility

Responsibility is the state of being responsible, accountable, or answerable. Teach children to be responsible, they will grow up to be responsible adults. Proverbs 22:6. Train up a child in the way he should go even when he is old, he will not depart. God said he chose Abraham because he trusted that he would train up his children (Genesis 18:19). Can God trust us like he did Abraham? Psalms 127:3. Children are the heritage of the Lord... God is eternal; his formula for insuring perpetuity is being fruitful and bringing up responsible children who will in turn become future parents responsible for bringing up their own children. This is rewarding for Him

Self-Control

Self-control must be taught. It is a key skill much needed for success in life. This helps to make appropriate decisions and respond to stressful situations in ways that can yield positive outcomes. Prov. 25:28. A man without self control is as defenseless as a city with broken down walls. Children should learn to delay gratification and be ruled by good and biblical principles. As a parent you should also practice self control because children mirror what you do. It is more effective when you do what you tell them to do. There is no parenting problem; if we experience any problem at all it is a wisdom problem. Christ has been made wisdom unto us. We can learn to tap into the wisdom of God every day as we raise our children. We must remember that wisdom is not an 'it'. Wisdom is a person, a supernatural being, Jesus. Teach them about the implication of wrongdoing to self, family and the society. Jesus will help you.

Invincibility

A lot of time children do not care about the implications of their actions especially the adolescents, they feel so invincible. They believe they cannot die or that nothing can happen to them. Teach the realities of physical laws (the laws that govern the universe), spiritual laws and even the societal laws. There are consequences for breaking these laws that can lead to injuries to self, others and the society at large, and even worse still, death. Children should, very early, learn to be law abiding. Begin with simple instructions from home.

Decision-Making

God wants us to be engaged rather than to be stuck in indecisiveness. There is no perfect solution, and the goal is not to avoid anything that has a speck of imperfection. To insist on perfection is to wait endlessly, because it is impossible. The goal is to live life to the full, doing as much as we possibly can even when it also embodies some flaws. No man is perfect except Jesus and we live our lives in Him. He is willing to overlook our weaknesses. Assure children that you can understand their weaknesses and mistakes and that's not really who they are; they can always outgrow any error and become stronger.

Let them know it is okay to make decisions even when it sometimes turns out to be wrong. It is totally unacceptable to NOT make a decision. One of the dangers of indecision is that you will be driven by the decisions of others. The bible describes such as a wave of the sea, being tossed up and down. This can affect every aspect of your life. Children should avoid having others make decisions for them. Also they should be careful of "herding" in which everybody is doing the same thing, it could be right or wrong, you just want to go with the decision of the majority. This does not show your individuality in decision making. Their decision should not be based on "because everybody is doing it". They should not be afraid or shy to stand alone. Standing alone is good, it shows your individuality. Just have a good reason for coming to that conclusion. It is better than not having any or joining the crowd. Avoid making decisions when angry, tired, or upset; you're most likely to make a wrong decision then. Any condition that would make you vulnerable should be avoided.

Pride

What is Pride?

It is an inwardly directed emotion that carries two meanings. One, with a negative connotation, pride refers to an inflated sense of one's personal worth or accomplishments. Two, with a positive connotation, pride refers to a positive sense of attachment towards one's own or another's choices. It is a product of praise, independent self-reflection, a fulfilled feeling of belonging. Children should be taught to know that we are who we are by the grace of Jesus Christ and we should always remember to give Him the glory. The word of God always portrays us in good light, and we should see ourselves that way. Doing something different is self-centeredness and a form of negative pride. Our boast should always be of the Lord, and who/what we are, and can become, in Him

Arrogance

Overbearing pride, evidenced by a superior manner towards others, unreasonable self-esteem, proud, contemptuous of others, haughty. Pride goes before destruction. Prov. 16:18. You should not praise yourself but allow others to do it but here is a word of caution: do not be moved by the praise of others, so that you will not to be affected by their criticism. Whatever you do, let it be to the glory of God. Arrogance makes you puffed up and encourages you look down on others. God hates it. It got Lucifer in trouble during his glorious days and he can never get out of it. Ezekiel chapter 28. In the same manner it will get any individual in trouble. People that are arrogant and prideful have problems submitting to authorities and this will go a long way to destroy them.

Discipline/Correction

Proverbs 22:6, train up a child…This is different from abuse and punishment. Anyone with abuse problem should seek help or be put away. With punishment: reaction is always greater than the offense but discipline, teaches what is acceptable. It is corrective.

Do not discipline in anger, it may amount to punishment. Punishment is always more than the amount of offence. Sometimes we do it in anger probably because we are embarrassed by their action or by some underlying conditions bothering the parent. If we are really embarrassed, we should think about how God Himself feels about the situation.

Start correction from home (charity begins at home). Not just outside. Don't make it seem acceptable at home and not acceptable outside; that is erratic, children get confused.

Train them both in love and justice. If you use love only and allow them to get away with all kinds of indulgences, they may not succeed in life. If you use justice only and are authoritative at all times, there will be lack of relationship and children may not develop properly. Overindulgence can kill or destroy the child. A child, left to himself, will bring shame… Prov.29:15. No matter how much you love this child, you should sum up courage to discipline him. If not, you are doing a disservice to him or her. You will ruin the child and his/her future. The discipline that you are not bold enough to give now will come later but in a hard way. The child would, most probably, punish himself psychologically in the future with guilt, self-hatred and all kinds of untold negative emotions, including depression. Such a child can end up in prison. You can save your child's future from such a nightmare, though he/she may not like it now but you will be his/her hero or heroine in the future.

A child left unguided or spending excessive time with TV is not likely to develop into a person of character, and may turn into a brat or monster. As you train your child, do it with caution. The bible encourages us to not provoke our children. Ephesians 6:4

Teaching Moments

Use everyday life issue to capture teaching moments. Allow the Holy Spirit to lead you. Don't be so stiff about the whole thing. Let it be as relaxed as possible. It should not be like being around you is like being in a military zone or boot camp, no relaxed moment. Allow the child to participate and express opinion in conversations. This will help you get a sense of what or how they are thinking. This will even help better to correct any erroneous mindset. Children are more relaxed when parents lovingly and clearly delineate the boundaries of acceptable behavior. Proverbs 19:18, encourages us to chastise while there is hope.

Diligence

The substance of a diligent is precious Prov. 12:27. Teach against waste. Even if you're very, very rich, avoid waste. Waste of money, materials, and more importantly, time. Give money in moderation, allow them to work and earn a living. For example, a billionaire couple were asked a question that was related to giving money to their children. The wife said they gave money weekly according to age, and that the children were also given household chores to match their age and capacity. This they do regularly. I also read about an American multimillionaire in oil business, got his children to start at the lowest level in his companies, even as attendants in his gas stations, as part of training for them. Ironically this person had friends that wanted him to employ their children (contemporaries of his children) as managers and directors, even when they are just fresh from school.

School and Communication

Find out about what goes on in school. Do your best to undo whatever was taught to them that was not really correct or that is against your values. Be involved with the school parent-teacher conferences and association. Check the homework, participate as needed. Provide necessary materials. Be there, be available for help, and be involved. As they grow older and go higher in school, your participation will be limited. Have an idea of what and how many classes they are taking, especially in college. The number of credits, how they are weighted, and what the classes are about. Find out, you may even be able to get enough information to have a meaningful conversation with them on these classes. Talk about their tests and quizzes and grades. Support them in making the right choices/decision about their educational advancement and career. Be careful not to impose your will on them. Remember, if both of you are leaning on God for direction, there should not be much disagreement in choices.

Harm reduction: Beware of harm reduction most of the time, it is not biblical, it's against Christian values. Examples; "It is ok to have sex as long as you use condom", "If you must do drugs, don't share needles" These things should not be done period.

Making Assumption

Assumption means taking things for granted, "supposing".

Teach children to ask questions and clarify issues. These will help to prevent problems.

Engage in activities that foster good communication with children. Examples: Sitting together at dinner table, sharing, discussing etc. all these invoke confidence and build communication skills. Think of other activities that bring family together and foster conversation, that allow every member to participate e.g. daily family altar, watching movies together.

Listening

It is Important to listen to children when they talk to you, listen to what they say as well as what they did not say. Sometimes they want to say what is half true so that they could get away with something. Do not pretend that you are listening when you are really not, they know when you are listening or not. Teach them how to listen also. Listen to them without judgment and without quick advice, as doing that will help them to develop more trust and confidence in returning to you for help. Don't dominate conversation, allow them to participate and ask questions. Teach them to listen more, talk less. Beware of anger and hasty talk. Proverbs 10:19 tells us that "in the multitude of words there wanted not sin, but he that refrained his lips is wise"

Speech

Avoid use of vulgar language and "cuss words." Most of these words revolve around body waste, sex and use of God's name. The first two are things that human beings do in privacy, only animals will not regard privacy. Using the name of God in vain is rejecting God's relationship and not honoring God.

We humans are created in the image and likeness of God. Swearing and using profanity is demeaning. Don't be too timid to reject vulgar language used around you. It is just not ok, and 1Cor15:33 makes it plain that "bad communication corrupts good manners".

Waywardness/Rebelliousness

Keep declaring the word of God concerning the child. It works, rest in the assurance that the word of God is true. Do not confess negative manifestation you see on the child but the promises of God concerning your children no matter how bad it looks. Seek help both physical and spiritual. Provide rehabilitation for a child that derailed and habilitation for the one that was never trained. You can always start or restart the training of a child. Seek professional help if needed.

Patience

Teach patience. Learn to delay gratification; more rewarding to wait than insisting on instant enjoyment which most of the time is short-lived.

Behavior

Commend good behavior and reward it. Condemn what is not acceptable, don't overlook it and think it will go away, do this as often as you can. May be you observe it at a show (like television) you are watching or even in other people, talk to them about the part that is good and the part that is not so good.

Obedience/Spiritual

Teach them to respect spiritual authority. Teach to obey simple instructions, don't explain things away. Use the happening around you as teaching opportunities, allow God to lead and direct you. I remember watching a movie a movie with my children when they were very young. One of the characters was told by the pastor not to participate in a secular music program. She got angry and threw the choir robe at the pastor and left.. My children were immediately told that throwing things at the pastor or someone that has authority over you or anyone for that matter is not okay. You may get angry but you must learn to control your behavior even in your anger.

When children have request or demands, saying no all the time may cause the child to rebel—ask God for wisdom to explain to the child. Of course there is a time to say "no." and you cannot say yes all the time either.

Energy in Wrong Direction

Help to redirect their energy to positive path. Apostle Paul, as Saul of Tarsus, (Acts 7 and 9) used his "zeal for God" to persecute Christians! After an encounter with Jesus, however, the same zeal was redirected to propagate Christianity even much more than any of the Apostles. Somebody that likes to talk, engaging in non-productive talk and gossips could be redirected to things that require talking in more productive ways e.g. teaching, not just at school, sales and marketing. Energy must be continually directed and focused to produce any useful result.

Forgiveness

Forgiveness is not by feeling, it's by faith and faith has nothing to do with feelings. It is different from reconciliation. You forgive because you were forgiven by Christ Jesus. Every single one of us were on our way to hell but because of Christ we have the hope of heaven. Look at the parable of the Unforgiving servant. Matthew 18: 21-35. People find it hard to forgive because they think it means they condone what the person did wrong or it means going back to relate with the person the way they were before the occurrence. This is not so. Trusting that person, and reconciling however, may take time or may never happen. Forgiveness is an act of faith and its commanded by Jesus. You can do all things through Christ that strengthens you. Be honest with yourself and in your prayer to God that you really don't feel like it but that you are calling on Jesus to help you and release the person and the situation to the hand of Christ. As you forgive the person through Christ, no matter how bad, Jesus Himself will heal the pain and the sorrow inflicted. If you do not do this you are doing the same thing to yourself over and over and the wound will never heal. Jesus can heal your heart regardless of how deep and terrible the wound is. That is just the way of the Lord, it is different from the way of man. Bitterness can harm you. I do not know your situation right now, forgiveness might just be the miracle that you have been waiting for. It will set you free, you will be amazed. There has been too many testimonies of healings, deliverances and breakthroughs that are connected with forgiveness. Do not allow the devil to take an advantage of you. Your refusal to forgive is like handing him an express ticket for an inroad into your life to commit atrocities whenever he wants it. Teach your children forgiveness also. Forgiveness Is a therapy or treatment that you give to yourself after you have been cheated or dealt with wrongly. You are not doing the person that offended you a favor, you are only taking care of yourself. You have the responsibility to do so. It is for your own good. Once you have done it, don't take it back, don't keep referring to it. If you do you are renting a space in your heart to that person, it is not worth it.

If you find yourself in sin, believe God to deliver you, keep on confessing your righteousness in Christ Jesus until you see the desired change in your life. The Bible says let the weak say I am strong.

Discernment

Discernment is a God given ability to spiritually sense between good and evil. This is different from suspicion. You discern with your spirit and suspect with your mind. Allow the spirit to guide you. Example; Looking at somebody's physical appearance or the person's way of dressing to judge is suspicion.

If you sense something is not right about your child, pray about it, bring it up immediately, avoid confrontation, have an open communication about it. If you feel uneasy about a relationship, especially your teenage ones warn them against it. Tell them to be careful, watch and pray. If they notice any sign that may confirm your feelings; they should not wish it away.

Asking for Their Rights

Teach them how to obtain and affirm their rights in a nice way, not being rude about it. You can be firm, persistent, in demanding what belongs to you without being confrontational or unruly. Resistance could be taken to God in prayer and victory will be delivered to you. For example, see the story of the daughters of Zelophehad in Numbers 27. They successfully changed God's rule and God was in agreement with them. In Hebrew culture, women did not have an inheritance, the father who was now dead had female children only, that means his portion will not be given to his children because of their gender. These women went to Moses being the leader of Israel at that time. Moses knowing there was no provision in the law for female children to inherit their father's property went to inquire of the Lord. The Lord told Moses to give them the inheritance. They won without strife and chaos.

Compliments

Do not do things so that you could be affirmed by others. You are already affirmed by God. He loves you. If you are given compliment for any action, accept it and give glory to God. Don't be moved by the praise of people so that you will not be disturbed by people's criticism.

Gossips

Teach children to avoid engaging in rumor mongering and gossips because, a lot of time, it is not really true to start with. It is easy to talk about other people. Backbiting, lately, has been channeled into more prominent ways such as tabloids and TV shows. People hardly know the characters personally, if at all, yet they talk about them even in games/sports. Our conversations should productive, edifying, creative, or inventive and innovative. Jesus is our example. "...*whatsoever* things are true, *whatsoever* things are honest, *whatsoever* things are just, *whatsoever* things are *pure*, *whatsoever* things are lovely, whatsoever things are of good report, if there be any virtue, if there be any praise, think on these things" Phil 4:8

Excessive Material

Providing excessive material stuff can lead to waste. Always have at the back of your mind that there are others that can use the excess. Whatever excesses you provide physically should also be matched with high level of spiritual development. Some parents like to say that they want to give what they lack when they were children because they can now afford them, unlike when they were growing up and their parents could not afford them. As you give them what you did not have, also give them what you had, such as good behavior, good habits, good work ethics, faith and discipline. In fact the bible says a good man leaves inheritance for his children and children's children. Prov.13:22. This should be viewed more in terms of non physical substances rather than material wealth. Think of strong Spiritual upbringing, discipline, education, good morals and virtue and values that are being handed down from generation to generation. Statistics shows that about 90 percent of the children of the rich and wealthy, who are not brought up to imbibe the diligence of the wealthy parents, end up mismanaging the inherited fortune.

Teach (and start this at early age) them what to do when they encounter friends and peers that like to show off excessive materials, brand name clothes, jewelries and accessories. Let them know their lives do not consist in what they have. Luke 12:15-20. You are not defined by what you have. The little that you have should be kept it in good shape, clean and tidy. Do not feel inferior because this is not who you really are, and no condition is permanent. If you are connected with God you will keep on experiencing positive changes.

Attitude

Bright and optimistic attitude will take anyone to higher heights. Teach children to be nice to themselves and people around them. Jesus is our ultimate hero, He is altogether lovely and we should really be like Him. In any situation children find themselves, they should learn to portray a good attitude. Ask what Jesus would do in that situation. In order to know what Jesus would do children need to be familiar with the bible and the teachings of our Lord Jesus Christ. Therefore as parents we need to be familiar with His teachings ourselves. (Get acquainted with the four gospels Matthew, Mark, Luke and John). Col.3:23 says "whatever you do, do it heartily as unto God not men". Having the right attitude can change a bad situation to a great one.

Formal Education

It is a major part of training. Invest in it, encourage it; just do all you can to make sure that they receive good education. Start saving early also, good education is not cheap. The world is advancing so fast that it's getting more and more difficult for illiterate or people without much education to catch up. With proper home training, and adequate formal education plus God on your side, you have what it takes to succeed in life.

Money

Money is a reward for what you do. The bible says "Do not muzzle an ox while it is treading the grain, the laborer deserves his wages" 1Cor.9:9. The oxen does not set out to go and eat, eating is what goes along with its treading. This means that meeting some needs, filling a gap is indirectly "setting out to make money" because money is mostly a reward for meeting the need of others. For example, medical doctors meet the need of sick people and get paid for the services provided. Mechanics meet the need of people by fixing broken cars and gets paid for meeting that need. As parents, you have responsibility to teach your children early to know where God is leading them and the type of people whose needs they are meant to meet and how to go about it and eventually, money will follow them.

Choosing a Career / Finding Your Niche

We have to have the mentality of service to humanity and teach that to our children. God created man after the Garden of Eden was already created, meaning that everything man needed was already in place. He commanded man to tend the garden, not so that they could make money or have food because they had everything they needed. When we provide service, there is a reward that follows, most of the time it is money and even something more important than money. Jesus our great example went about doing good and His fame went abroad. He did not set out for fame. He saw the need and met it. (Read the whole account in the Bible Gospels, Matthew, Mark, Luke, and John)

Some people have suggested that, in choosing a career that children need to choose what they love to do. It is not always about what they love to do. You don't always get paid for what you love to do. For example, I have seen people that like to gaze at stars and other heavenly bodies at night. I don't know how much they can get paid to do that. But hey, this is their hobby, they enjoy it but I bet they have some sure source of income. Of course you can carve a business or career around what you like, but it is not always possible. People have all kinds of strange hobbies and pastimes that they love and would rather do at all time if it is possible. They will not always get paid for it. I once heard someone who said he loved boating, adding that nobody had ever offered to pay him for his more-than-20-years love for boating.

If you choose an area to meet needs, you can always develop a love for it. When you are helping others to reach their goals, there is always a reward, be it monetary and fulfillment. When you get into it, you may need to develop the skill for it. With God given grace, you will excel in ways that others would benefit from and would be willing to pay you for it.

I met a lawyer when I had some court issues. The way she spoke and explained things would make me to be at peace and relaxed. I felt like I was in the presence of God every time I spoke with her. She was amazing. She did the initial part of the case, she could not continue because the case progressed and escalated to another level. She did her best to find someone she trusted for me. I was willing to pay for her to stay on the case, but she declined, stating that she had never handled that type of case at that higher level. She thought I had a good chance to win and did not want to ruin my chance. For her it was not about making money. It was about helping me and her other clients. Clients described her as a gem/angel. God bless her heart.

Don't get confused; don't allow peers and environmental circumstances to influence your decision. Parents should avoid forcing a niche on any child. Pray and allow God to guide you. Find that need and be the one that meets the need, that's your niche. You don't have to love it in the beginning. Your compassion for the people will generate the love eventually. Your destiny is tied to some other people's destiny in helping them to reach their goals.

Borrowing

Children should be instructed to avoid borrowing; they must understand the implication and what it does to people. In our society the use of credit cards is widely accepted, children must learn as they grow up and become more and more accountable, that they don't have to live a lifestyle of debt. In proverbs 22:7 the word of God says "the rich rules over the poor and the borrower is servant to the lender". Rom 13:8 even urges us to "owe no man, nothing but to love…" Deut. 15:6. You shall not borrow but lend unto nations. Let them know that the word of

God is the truth and we can live debt-free. As parents, our goal is to lead by example and do everything to get out of debt if we have not done so.

We should find simple ways to pass this instruction across to them at whatever level they are. For example, one of my daughters was around 6 years old. We got a carton of juice boxes containing about 36 boxes. We told her, along with her siblings, to have one juice box each per day; no more, because we wanted to make sure that they drank water instead of depending on juice. Moreover, it was healthier and economical. One day that daughter decided to drink two boxes of juice instead of one. When we asked her why she did that, she immediately said, oh I'll skip tomorrow. She was quickly informed that it was not that easy. Life does not always work like that. First she was disobedient, which was wrong and so she needed to reflect on that. Second, she drank two instead of one. It was just like borrowing. She felt like she wanted a second one instead of only one, and decided to drink that of tomorrow today. It's like she borrowed the juice box of tomorrow for today. She was told that in real life, when you borrow, you pay interest and fees. You end up paying several times more than what you borrowed. So we told her that she would not just skip one day but 3 days being part of interest, fees and penalties. She understood the logic, hopefully would take it with her and avoid borrowing unnecessarily when she grows up. Borrowing makes you lose your future revenue. You mortgaged your future.

Limit the use of credit cards. If you cannot afford it now, you probably should not get it now. Save for it and buy later. It is good to delay gratification now for a better future. The negative effect of huge credit card debt is not just about the individual, it affects the whole society at large. Avoid unnecessary debt. Learn to save money. Buy only what you need. Avoid being wasteful. Think about those who do not have.

Savings and Investment

Teach savings early, it could be hard to do initially, it takes getting used to, learn to make it a lifestyle. As you give tithe in church and give to others learn to save ten percent for yourself, before you know it, it adds up. Think about the use of piggy bank and eventually the bank account with interest. It might be little, it is something. Teach investment, especially in something secure. Our LORD Jesus endorses investments, you can see that from the parable of the Talent or Minas Matt.25:14-30. The least of all these suggested investment was to take it to the bank to yield interest. The book The Richest Man in Babylon by George Samuel Clason contains nuggets about how to save, make money and invest. You may want to look into it for examples.

Raise your children to be entrepreneurs. They are better prepared to face life than children being raised to become employees. Your entrepreneurial oriented child would grow up seeing business almost everywhere while your non entrepreneurial child would always be looking for where to find job and impress his employer. Teach them leadership principles and public speaking. Encourage creativity. They must never be too proud to ask for help, everybody needs a little help sometimes. Seek to know God in all your doings. He is the very present help in time of needs. Learn to depend on Him at all times. Rest in Him when things are bad. Lean on Him when things are good, with Him your good things will become better and continue to greatness. There is no limit to how much we should depend on Him. Make it a lifestyle and a lifetime of commitment.

Giving and Sharing

Give your life to Jesus. Make Him your Lord and Savior. Give yourself to God in relationship and in service unto Him. Teach children in giving to church and to others. It helps in the furtherance of the Kingdom of God and in helping the less privileged. The Bible encourages it. Mal 3:10. Bring your tithe to my store house... He that gives to the poor lends onto God, He will repay. Proverb 19:17. Even the government encourages giving by giving tax breaks for most giving. Apart from the tax break, it is a spiritual issue. God commanded it for our own good. The earth was cursed after the fall of man. When you bring a portion of your income which is the tenth to the church, it is a way of exemption from the curse upon the earth. You as a person have been redeemed by the blood of Jesus Christ. It is also a test of our obedience. If God says bring it just do it. As soon as children can understand, teach them to give. If someone gives them a dollar, let them know to give ten cents. It is a good practice to grow with and they get used to it.

In conclusion, training should be life-long. Children who have grown should continue self-training and personal development as adults. So, which means parents should continue to lead in these examples. There are training programs, studying the word of God as the number one, seminars, webinars, etc. on interesting and relevant topics. Get on these things and let's keep getting better.

The Bible implores us to train our children. It also assures us that they will yield especially if we start early. It is a simple instruction. The process should not be stressful to either the parents or the children. Anything short of that is a problem that requires an intervention. It may be necessary to seek professional help, but first and foremost, it is important to seek spiritual help. The child or the parent may be demonically oppressed (in this case you need the help of a deliverance minister), they may be suffering from the negative influence of generational curses and many other things. You can easily identify these things when you see a negative patterns of incidence and occurrences like sickness, failure, psychopathic behavior etc. If its looking out of the ordinary, there is probably an underlying spiritual causative factor involved, do something about it. Do not wish it away and think its one of those things. Get help right away. As you continue in prayer and relationship with God, you will experience victory more and more in every area of your life.

Chapter 4

Relationships

This is simply how to relate with others. It may be divided into two. First to God and second to man (Self, family, friends, neighbors and the society at large) Your #1 relationship is with God.

Children must be raised in the fear and honor of God. There are serious consequences if we fail at these responsibilities. There is also a reward for doing it and more reward for doing it well. Prophet Eli and his sons, check the story from 1 Sam.2 in the bible. This is an example of people who did not honor God and their lives ended in a terrible manner. God said of Abraham that He trust him (Abraham) to bring up his children in the way of the Lord.Gen.18:19, Jonadab Jer.35:6 is another good example. If your relationship with God is important to you, you cannot hide your faith. Jesus says "if you are ashamed of me, I will also be ashamed of you in the presence of my father" If you accept Jesus, He lives His life through you, but abandoning your relationship with

God will lead to moral decadence because He is the source of good morals. Without God people cast off restraints.

King Solomon made this error towards the end of his life. We read in the bible that the multiple women that he has, stole his heart away from God. He started well and ended not so well. We must stay connected to God at all times.

Your second relationship is with man. First is your relationship with yourself, then with family, friends, neighbors and the society at large. Relating with your self is important, teach children how to do this, they need to know who they are, love and value themselves, love what they have and hope for the better. When a mistake or an error is committed, ask God for forgiveness, make your mind up to prevent a repeat of such, forgive yourself and move on. Loving self helps to reduce poor self esteem and poor self concept. Know who you allow into their lives. Many stories of abuse especially sex abuse happen with people you know. In fact statistics show that first sexual encounters happen with people that are in the home or commonly visit the home, i.e. Friends of brother, father, uncle.

Learn to relate with people, not electronic games and not much of the newer technologies. Forgive others as quickly as possible. People are not perfect just like you are not. Otherwise, the whole world would soon become your enemy because your expectation of people is too high and your demand of them is not easily met and so you get easily offended. You just need to learn how to deal with people within the limitation of their behavior

When the children are no longer living together, maybe they are off to college, or have moved on to different areas. Be the one in the middle, connecting them together, makings sure that they connect with each other and you regularly. There is strength in numbers, make sure that your children stick together in love when they are still at home with you and let them continue when they are no longer with you..

Friends

Choose friends that replenish you and not deplete life out of you. Notice how you feel or what you sense when you relate with some people. Also, be the friend that will influence others positively. Be strong and stand your ground for what is right. With time you will win them over.

Sex

Talk clearly about sex at the appropriate time. As a parent don't be too shy about it. Don't be proverbial about it. In school, they talk about it, they teach them. They even give out condoms. Why should you not want to talk about it? Teach clearly that sex is meant for marriage according to the bible. Although people do it outside marriage but it is not the biblical way. It is a gift from God for intimacy. It brings about procreation. The bible calls premarital sex fornication and when it involves a married person outside of marriage it is adultery. Not being clear of your conversation with your child about sex is not good, and it is even worse when not discussed at all. I have heard of a story of someone who told her daughter it is wrong to kiss a boy and warned her strongly about kissing without stressing to avoid sex. The daughter became pregnant, when the mother confronted her she said "mommy you told me not kiss, I never kissed him." Kissing does not lead to pregnancy; it is the real sex, Teach children that though it is not in vogue to abstain from sex, it is still godly and biblical. They should not be shy to stand above it.

See the example of Joseph in the book of Genesis 39. He was about to be to be lured by Potiphar's wife, he fled. He said he would not sin against God. When King David fell with the sin of adultery, he said he sinned against God Psalms 51. Sex outside marriage is a sin against God. Beware of people who want to use you for sex. Some are "unfriendly friends" because they are not true friends. They do not have your best interest in mind. They want to pimp you for money, drugs or other kinds of favors. Some really want to let you know that they like you, or even love you, but it's just for sex. If they truly love you, they would wait for you. Do not be deceived it could be both ways (male or female). If you do this, you are doing it against your own body Prov. 6:32-34. You can never get it back. Avoid inflicting psychological wound that will be difficult to heal on yourself and others. You may also have friends who are already doing it and want you to join them. Do not join them it is okay to stand alone on this. You may lose your friendship with such but you are standing for what is right.

Beware of pedophiles. Many are sheep in wolfs clothing. It was noted that they like to prey churches. One of them was interviewed on why they do it in churches. He said "church people are quick to trust and quick to forgive." Once they come into church and claim they are Christians, members welcome them with open arms and let down their guards. Even after they commit their atrocities, they may not be reported for actions to be taken because the Christian doctrines preach forgiveness. Statistics show that the first sexual encounters happen with people the child knows (not necessarily in love relationship with). Many times it happens in their own homes. They are family members, friends of family, mother's boyfriend, or neighbors. Be sensitive, not suspicious, but do not be too trusting.If it doesn't feel right. It is probably not right. Trust your intuition. You could have been warned before it happened. If you respond to the nudging from within and take cautions, it wills spare everybody a lot of trouble.

Family Dynamics

This refers to the ways in which family members relate to one another. It should be healthy. According to the bible, the father is the leader while the mother is the co leader. The mother should be careful to not take over the role of the father either intentionally or unintentionally. The father must not neglect his role either. The family value should be Jesus centered. In Him, Jesus Christ, all things consist. For In him we live, and move and have our being. Acts17:28. Both father and mother set the rule of the house and train the children to comply. Parents should live by examples. The members are individuals with unique personality and behave differently, abiding by the rules help members to function in harmony.

Team Efforts and Working Together. Let your family dynamics be healthy. Let the children know we complement one another to function as one family unit rather than being in competition with one another. Teach the importance of working together towards the same goal. They must understand that helping each other helps in moving the family forward. Raise them as one family who is part of a larger group or subculture e.g. church, extended family etc. This creates a sense of belonging and networking that helps to function better in the larger society,

Household chores

Allow participation as soon as they can. Assign task in proportion to individual age and maturity. I listened to an interview on the television. It was one of the billionaire in America, with the wife, they explained how they assigned their children with household chores and pay them weekly as their earnings. The reporter showed some level of surprise and asked them a follow up question as to why they don't lavish their children with money. These multi billionaires answered that the children must learn how to make money.

Individuality

Each child is unique and different. Observe and study their individuality and unique personality. Deal with them as individuals and raise them together with their uniqueness in mind. This will help their relationship with the parents and reduce conflicts.

Family Secret

Family secret could be something good or bad that we don't really want to share with outsiders. Sometimes it is a trade secret or a secret recipe that makes your product stand out above your competitors. A lot of time they are embarrassing issues in the family called "family secret." We need to handle such with wisdom. Have an open communication with the family members and clear their minds. Explain the exact issues and let it be clear to everybody. Let children know that God understands. If it something that requires forgiveness. God is willing to forgive. We also need to forgive ourselves and move forward. Whatever is happening within the family, know that bigger or more serious issues have happened, or are happening somewhere else. It is not the worst case in the world and certainly not, the end of the world.

I was listening to a man on Christian TV whose wife got pregnant out of wedlock and they were keeping the baby in the family. She and her husband explained what happened in a way that the children would understand. They added that mummy is sorry about what happened and God had forgiven her and the rest of the family would have to accept it. If there is a member with disability, learn to accept it and educate yourselves about the issue. Support this member, it will make it easy for everyone

Sibling Rivalry

It is a type of animosity or competition among children, blood related or not. Biblical examples-Abel and Cain, Esau and Jacob. Children are sensitive to parental treatment. You do not want to create enmity between your kids. Parents can reduce the opportunity for rivalry by refusing to compare or give preferential treatment to their children. Teach the children positive ways to get attention from each other and the parent. Plan fun family activities together and make sure each child has enough time and space of their own. A good example is family altar session. If well handled it affords everyone the opportunity to participate–equal assignment, equal opportunity to talk and contribute. Parents can also give each child individual attention, encourage their work. For example, Noah and son built the ark. Refuse to hold up a child as a role model for other, avoid favoritism, ex: Joseph and father, Esau and Jacobs's mother

Sibling rivalry could be very frustrating and stressful to parents. Physical and emotional changes, cause pressure in the teenage years. This may also happen during adulthood. Try to nip this in the bud at an early age. Believe God to hold you all together to him. In Him we live…Act 17:28. Make Jesus the center of your focus and He will hold you all together. It cuts across culture and may lead to serious issue including sibling abuse if not dealt with. Murder has been reported in some cases. Long time ago, I read a book where the family had no wood to heat the house. One sibling suggested that the family should use the newborn as wood. Prevention should begin even before another child comes. Always prepare the mind of the first child, that there will be multiple children in the home and that he/she would have sisters and brothers. As soon as pregnancy comes tell the existing child about it. This will foster positive expectations. When the new one comes, allow the older one to participate in the care of the newborn in his/her little way with supervision. Don't neglect him or her.

Chapter 5

Christian Faith

Christian (Bible) faith is the belief in the Almighty God, the creator of heaven and earth who loves us so much that He gave us His only begotten Son, Jesus Christ. Jesus Himself loves us and gave his life for us. Parents need to have that understanding and teach it to the children. Man is a spirit being who lives in a body and has a soul. The soul is the seat of the emotion and with the body we interact with the environment. The only way we could access our spirit which is the real us is by the word of God. Needless to say that studying and knowing the word of God is very important, that is the only way to know who you really are. We cannot be ruled by our feelings or be dominated by our moods but rather by the word of God, the bible. Of course it is okay to express how we feel but we should not be bound by these feelings.

Religious beliefs

Nowadays, it is common to hear statements such as, "I am not religious, or I am not a fanatic, or I am just a nominal Christian." If you are a true Christian, you better stand for what you believe, and who you believe. Apostle Paul says that for I know whom I have believed and I am fully persuaded... 2 Tim 1:12 Let the children know they are kings and the children of the most high. They have the seed of greatness in them. In fact the bible says in Psalms 82:6 "Ye are gods, and all of you are children of the most High" As early as possible, they should learn to walk with the mindset that they are destined for greatness. It is not acceptable for them to talk "trash", dress "trash", or behave "trash" because that is not the norm for great people Teach them to not be apologetic about their faith. If somebody asks them if they are Christian, let them know it is okay to say yes. Jesus said whosoever denies Him in the public, such He would deny before His Father. Teach them to understand the Christian faith and what it's all about. If they do not understand, they will easily accept what others sell for them. Christian were first referred to as Christian by unbelievers at Antioch because they were Christ-like in behavior and character. The bible says by their fruit you shall know them. In the book of John chapter 3 Jesus Himself says we must be born again in order to have eternal life. Jesus went further to describe what is eternal life in John 17:3, "And this is life eternal, that they might know thee, the only true God, and Jesus Christ whom thou hast sent". All we need to do is to come to Jesus as we are, ask Him to forgive our sins, accept and believe in His redemptive work and surrender to Him as our Lord and Savior. He will accept us and give us His Spirit and make the Holy Spirit to dwell in us. This is His grace, we do nothing to deserve it. God is no longer angry with man, He wants to reconcile with man through His son Jesus Christ out of His deep love for us. John 3:16

Knowing Jesus

Knowing Jesus is our greatest blessing. He encompasses everything. In Him all things consist. He has given us all things through the knowledge of Him. Knowing this truth as a parent helps us to do a successful job of raising godly children and teaching this truth help them to navigate through life successfully.

One of the best type of education you can give to your child is the knowledge of Jesus because you are not always going to be present with them. Knowing Jesus makes them develop the inner fortitude to resist every temptation. Example is Joseph. See Genesis chapters 37-50 Joseph was far away from home and away from his parents. He had the strength to resist the temptation of Portiphar's wife. Joseph said "how can I do this and sin against God". The sin of fornication or adultery is a sin against God. When they learn to honor God, God will honor them. Training them and ensuring that they know Jesus will also help them have the inward strength to be different from others. While others are ordinary, they will be extraordinary. While others seek man's approval, they will first seek God's approval and eventually they will be approved of men. Examples are, Daniel, Joseph, Esther, etc.

Word of God

Teach them early to meditate on the word of God, commit it to memory apply it daily. Don't think they are too young. The devil does not think they are too young, when he is ready to afflict them. Focusing on the word puts them on the path for life style of miracles. You can encourage one scripture or one verse per week. Give rewards for each verse they successfully memorized and teach them how they apply what has been committed to memory. Please note that memorizing a word is just at the lowest level. Your focus should be more on meditation whereby you create a the picture of this word in your mind and you paint it over and over in your heart until it becomes so real to you. At this level it becomes so tangible that it flows through your mouth from your heart as your confession/profession. "For out of the abundance of the heart, the mouth speaketh". Merely repeating the word from memory becomes more like parakeeting. It is not about the volume but the quality. Meditation on the word of God exposes you to its quality and the effectiveness which helps you to stand in the face of adversity.

Fear anxiety/issue

Don't raise your children in fear, thinking that evils of society (social ills) will befall them. That is living in fear. "Job said the things that I fear came upon me" I remember attending a discussion forum of some Christian women, and one of them suggested that parents must be careful, and if possible, move children from the inner city to the suburbs because of drugs, gangs, etc I made bold to tell her that raising kids was not just about location. It is first about Jesus, and when you have Jesus as your foundation, you can now start building on Him. Responding to the lady, I said in the forum that "if drugs are like snowflakes or dusts on the streets of the city, they will not cling to my children's shoes talk less of them touching it" I strongly believe in psalm 91… He that dwells in the secret place of the most high shall abide under the shadow…" And I know whom I have believed and I am fully persuaded that He is able to keep that which I have committed unto his hands. Today, to Him be all the glory forever and forever concerning my children.

Going to church

Don't just send them to church. Take them to church. The center of your children's life is Jesus; everything else follows. The child should go to church with you. They may not like it now they will thank you for it in the future. Watching Christian program on the TV or internet is not exactly the same as going to church.

You may participate if you join online or TV services, participating is a little more involving than watching. There is a corporate anointing that you miss out on when you stay at home. Hebrew 10:25-27 encourages us "not forsaking the assembly of ourselves together". Hebrew 12:22 See what the bible says takes place in Mt Zion (church). If you don't like your church, go to another but be sure that your move is by the leading of God. It is not a good idea to stay home just because somebody "offended" you. You are the one losing out.

Doing Good

Do not be weary of doing well. We also learn from Joseph in prison that it pays to do well at all times wherever we find ourselves. Joseph in prison interpreted dreams for fellow inmates from Pharaoh's palace and caused him to be remembered in the king's palace. Thus while he was still in prison, he continued to use his talent and that eventually paved the way for his lifting.

Disobedience

If your child is rebellious, correct him for a good reason, not just to save your face or to save you from embarrassment. It should not be about you or how you feel but about the destiny of the child in God. Children are the heritage of the Lord. They belong to God. Before you think about how you feel, think about how God feels. He too has feelings, we are his children. He loves us, think about what it feels like to hurt someone you love or someone you love hurts you. God is willing to forgive them quickly. In truth Jesus paid for their sins already

Submissiveness to parents

Teach the importance of submissiveness; Jesus was submissive to his earthly parent. He has the power to rebel, but he did not. The bible says he grew in stature and wisdom. Honor your parents (and elders) and people in authority. The bible says your days will be lengthened. They are biblical principles.

Being Jesus Centered

As we behold Jesus more and more, we become like Him. We are the epistle that the world is reading. Children should be taught to focus more on Jesus in everything they do. Reading the four Gospels frequently will help them to do this more effectively.

Prayer and Declaration of Blessings

What is Prayer?

There are so many definitions and descriptions of prayer that may be found in the Bible, teachings on tapes and books. One of the most important thing is for us to know that prayer is not a monologue where you are the one doing all the talk, but a dialogue between you and God. It is an actual communication between the two of you. As you speak to Him, you have to listen to Him speak back to you. It should be noted also that He communicates with you in many ways apart from speaking. A preacher humorously put it this way, that God understands English but English is not His primary language. The Bible teaches that we must pray always. That means in every situation and circumstances, good or bad, we must stay in prayer. Our Lord Jesus is our great example. Luke 5:16. The Bible shows that He prays always. If Jesus prayed that much, how much more should we pray? too much more, which can never be enough. For example if you are in good health, you pray to remain in good health. If you are in sickness, you pray to be healed. If you are successful, you pray not to be selfish and if you are prosperous you pray not to be proud, even in sorrow, you pray not to be cynical. the list can go on and on. And so in raising your children you pray that God should help you to do it successfully. If you do not know how to pray, you start by praying to God to teach you how to pray. See the disciples examples.These disciples were with Jesus all the time, they still had to go to Him to teach them how to pray. We can always learn from their examples. Jesus said he can do nothing except what he sees His Father doeth. John 5:19-20 We have to surrender totally to God in prayer and listen to Him for instructions on how to take care of our children. The common excuse that people give when prayer is suggested is that they do not have the time to do it. You need to create the time, Jesus was busy in His earthly ministry, He created the time to go meet with His Father in prayer. In Luke 5:16. The bible says

He will slip away into the wilderness to pray. I like the title of a book on Prayer "Too Busy Not to Pray". It's like the more busy you are, the more you need to pray. If you invest time into praying, you redeem more time in your daily activities. You get a lot more done. You work smart and achieve more than just working hard. Hard work is good and most time very rewarding, but even more rewarding is when you apply prayer and the wisdom of God on your hard work. It is also important for you to get into the habit of practicing His Presence throughout the day consciously knowing that He's there with you. Get settled with God and the Holy Spirit to a lifetime of commitment of a deep relationship that will give you guidance and counseling in every aspect of your life and particularly in child rearing.

Consider being baptized in the Holy Spirit with the evidence of Speaking in tongues. Speaking in tongues which is also praying in the Spirit is the prayer of the new Testament. I know some people have a problem with this. Do your research on this. Testimonies abound everywhere concerning the effectiveness of speaking in tongues. 1 Cor.14:2. Ephesians 6:18. Do not allow the devil to take an advantage of you as a result of doctrines. Jesus Himself said "in my Name they shall…..speak with new tongues……." Mark 16:17. If Jesus said it why are you not doing it. Ask the Holy Spirit to baptize you and begin to speak in tongue in Jesus Name. Receive in faith and speak. You are probably the only one left. The people with whom you probably discussed against speaking in tongue have all started speaking in the "new tongues", they just did not inform you.

The power of the tongue, Proverbs 18:21 is engaged in declaration of blessings. Whatever you do not want to happen in your life, do not say it with your mouth, it is that simple. The Bible says "say not before an Angel it was an error" Eccl.5:6. Parents need to make it a duty to declare blessings upon their children from time to time. There are some cultures that pray on their children and declare blessings at particular phases of life. An example is the Jewish culture. It has been proven that the Jews are one of the successful if not the most successful group of people in the world today. Check the statistics in every area of life, Science breakthroughs, business, major inventions, Nobel Laureates, they have truly been a blessing to the world. There are seven stages of life when Jewish parents will declare blessings on their children. The stage of conception, period in the womb, stage of birth, period of infancy and childhood, period of puberty and adolescent. time of marriage and old age. It is said that the blessings may be repeated several times during each period until the child grows up to the next stage. It was said that the prayer may be repeated multiple times per day. You will say the blessing declaration of the current phase and keep repeating it until child reaches another phase. I believe we can all copy this to our advantage, from conception to the adult life when it will now be their turn to start blessing us. Begin to declare right from when you tested positive and do this continually every day and if possible multiples time daily. Example You can make declaration as follows: Child (Insert name once they have a name) The Spirit of excellence rest upon you and dwells in you. As you grow in stature, you grow up in the wisdom of God. The blessing of God is upon you and you enjoy favor with God and man. God Almighty is your defense every day of your life. You are a blessing to people around you and the world at large. (Please note that this a suggestion like the rest of this writing, I believe you will do yourself and your child a favor if you make use of some of the suggestions. For additional reading, you may see "The Power of a Parents Blessing by Craig Hill.

These simple declarations are what Joseph Prince called-Earnest Prayer which he described as a simple declaration of faith. The Bible tells us that when Elijah prayed earnestly that it would not rain, it did not rain on the land for three years. 1 King 17:1. All Elijah did was made a simple declaration. You decide on what you want and believe that God will make it happen of course it has to be in line with the will of God and then declare it with your mouth. Your simple confession of faith is more powerful when you are deeply rooted in the word of God and resting in the finished work of Jesus on the cross and His resurrection, so get on board. Teach children to declare positively with their mouth. It is a "cool" thing to do. It may not be cool among friends in school or social cycles. It is cool for their life. You may also check Kerry Kirkwood's book "The Power of Blessing" for more.

Dreams

Encourage them to share their dreams. Pray with them if they have a scary dream or nightmare. Allow the Holy Spirit to interpret their dreams. Pray a simple prayer for interpretation. If they have a dream that is not clear or they forget, pray that they get another one that can explain the first one, clearer and better. Jesus said my sheep hears my voice. God will always speak to us in the language that we understand. God visits us in our dreams to instruct, direct and prevent us from falling into error and sin (Job 33:14-18).

There are so many examples of God leading by dreams in the bible. God led Joseph to not leave his wife Mary when she found her with a child. Matthew 1:20. The covenant that God cut with Abraham was in the book of Genesis was in a dream. A lot of people do not believe in this, that does not make it wrong. It is a good resource that God has given us, it should not be neglected.

Book of Proverbs-book of wisdom

We have all heard of an apple a day keeps the Doctor away; let's do a proverb a day to keep folly away. The book of Proverb is made up of 31 chapters, one for each day of the month. Each chapter is loaded with words of wisdom that will help us through life. As parents use them and lets help children grow up in using them. Testimonies abound about people who have increased in wisdom because of meditating on the book of proverbs.

There are great testimonies about people with low IQ that became significantly improved after a habit of feeding and meditating on this book of wisdom.

Family Altar

A great avenue for family members to fellowship together and commune with God as a group, it is like a little church you run in your home as often as you do it. It serves as a way of communication as a group also as an opportunity to learn from each other and express oneself. When we come together as a family in the unity of mind to commune with God and express ourselves in prayer, it is powerful. Make it interesting, do not make it too formal

Encourage participation of each member example, bible reading, leading prayer, teaching etc. Have a fixed time that is convenient as much as possible for everybody. Be creative about it. Make it very practical. Allow time for questions and answers. You may study any Christian book of interest together, or listen to tapes or short Christian movie but more importantly the Bible.

As much as possible don't make it a time to discuss what a family member has done wrong and how such should be reprimanded. It is a sacred time between your family and God. It is a time that the Holy Spirit can teach you together as a group. We started when my children were young, they looked forward to it, growing up they love it and have expressed their desire to continue it in their own home when the time comes.

Bible

Every member should have at least one, even before they start reading. Buy one suitable for the age. It could be picture bible they will grow up to cherish their bible and the word of God. Let everyone carry his/her bible to church, including the picture bible. You should see it as a must for every member. Get one for the baby too as you carry him or her, carry his or her bible too, it is symbolic.

Relationship with the Holy Spirit

The Holy Spirit is the third Person of the Trinity. It is important to get into a relationship with the Holy Spirit because by Him we know the Father. Knowing the Father helps us to know the love of the Father. Being baptized in His love help us to overcome fatherless mentality and deliverance from the orphan spirit. Jesus Himself said to His disciples when He was wrapping up His earthly ministry that the Holy Spirit who is the Comforter will teach us all things. John 14:26. He is described as a Helper, Counselor, Teacher, Intercessor, Advocate, Strengthener and much more. When you get into an intimate relationship with Him, He reveals Himself to you in a personal way that you will have your own functional special Name for Him but this must be born out of communion and intimacy with Him. Jesus wants us to do this because the Holy Spirit is the one that can truly reveal Christ to us. He dwells in us and we must be conscious of His presence in us and relates with him just like anybody else. Talk to Him and listen to Him talk back. (This may not necessarily be an audible voice, it may be an impression in your mind). This is going to make some people uncomfortable but if Jesus says we need this relationship, you really need to believe it. He is a gentleman and would not force Himself on you, you have to be the one that would initiate an ongoing communication with Him. He is willing and happy to respond. The bible says He will guide you into all truth. if you are not in fellowship with Him you cannot receive guidance. The world is becoming more and more a dangerous place, it will be dangerous to navigate your way around without the guidance of the Holy Spirit. Jesus Knows what its going to be like when He gave us the Gift of the Holy Spirit. it is left for us to take advantage of the ministry of the Holy Spirit. He helps us in our prayer and in decision making. This is when we engage Him in listening prayer but always be sure that your listening prayer is born out of your relationship with Him.

If you only go to Him just to know His mind when you are having a difficulty or want to make a decision, it becomes something like divination, you cannot do that to the Holy Spirit. He is God. Engage in the practice of the presence of the Holy Spirit and teach your children to do the same. See John Bevere's book "The Holy Spirit" for more. You also need to engage in listening prayer and teach your children how to do it. Teach children to be still quiet down, hear God speak with them, God is great. He speaks in a still small voice. If we as parents have not learned this then we must learn it and impart it to our children as well. It is very helpful in decision making. Mary Ruth Swope's book on listening prayer (How to hear from God) is a recommended book on the subject. Teach how to listen to God, tune in. He speaks with still small voice. He speaks in pictures, impressions and others. It is actually easy to hear, but your must learn and practice how to. Some call it simple prayer. You stay still expecting Him to talk to you regarding an issue, He will. It is not every time you practice listening prayer that you are asking for something, sometime you just want to sit and enjoy fellowship with Him just listening. He speaks through the word. Read and study the scriptures.

Belief and Thought

As a man thinks in his heart so is he Prov.23:7

Thought is important, thought is impactful. What is even more impactful is the belief behind your thought. Your belief drives your thought. Watch your own thinking habit; it is to you according to your thinking. Job said "what I feared came..." He was always thinking horror, fear, anxiety, and then it came to pass. If you know the word of God and allow it to form the basis of your belief, this will drive your thinking in the right direction making it possible for you to live right. Do it as a parent and teach children to do the same. Teach them

Godly thought especially concerning the promises of God for His children on prosperity, divine health, protection, divine direction etc. Do not think they are too young, that should be the more reason for you to be committed because the impressionable age is the most vulnerable period. Observe your emotion, if it is not so great, you will be able to trace it to your thought and belief. Belief in God's love for you and let the children know that God truly loves them more than anyone or anything else in this world.

Chapter 6

Conclusion

Entropy is a term used in science to describe lack of order or predictability. It means gradual decline into disorder and chaos. A few synonyms of this word are deterioration, degradation, decline, crumbling, degeneration and others. Any of these words could be used to describe the status or the natural order of things in the material world when left without care or maintenance. Simply put, when something is not being taken care of, it is being neglected. With neglect comes breaking down, collapse, decay and destruction. Such is the potential picture of children left untrained. These types of children will be destroyed and could even destroy others with them. They become societal problems and burdens. The bible says a child left to himself brings shame to his mother. Prov.29:15. We have the responsibility to intervene by taking actions just like we take care of our material things such as vehicles, houses and many other possessions.

To intervene means to interfere or stop the natural cause of decay or destruction which is the default. Without intervention, things go downward spiral and destruction is inevitable. Interventions in raising children involve physical care, training, prayer, trusting God and many more. Some were previously discussed and some are not mentioned in this book. Allow the Holy Spirit to guide you. We must take the job of raising our children seriously and ask God to help us. An average parent wants to keep his/her children happy. While this is considered acceptable, parents should bear in mind, that if instructions, training, and discipline, are sacrificed for happiness, these children will become likely candidates for unhappiness and deep sorrow in the future. A little drift away from acceptable values here and there, which may appear negligible at the time, may add up as disaster many years later. This may cause irreparable loss and damage. Therefore, be very careful when it comes to compromising your stand as a parent. You don't want your child getting in trouble with law or ever missing God's purpose for his or her life.

When a child is born, he is born innocent, ignorant and immature. As we take steps, some of which were mentioned above, children grow up to become responsible adults, who will also take care of their young ones and leave the world a better place than they met it. Consider our Lord Jesus Christ who is fully God, was also fully man during His time on earth had to grow up in stature and wisdom and His fame went abroad. Luke 2:40, Luke 2:52. The bible says of Jesus in the book of Isaiah 9:6 "For unto us a child is born, unto us a son is given...." When a **child** is born to us, let us align ourselves with Godly principles instilling values that will mold the child to become a **son/daughter** who will be given to the world as a gift that changes their world. Such son/daughter, as an adult, will daily walk with the conviction of maintaining and raising the standards that have been imparted to him or her through the biblical principles.

Printed in the United States
By Bookmasters